Rainforest Colors

Susan Canizares • **Betsey Chessen**

SCHOLASTIC INC.

NEW YORK • TORONTO • LONDON • AUCKLAND • SYDNEY

Acknowledgments

Science Consultants: Patrick R. Thomas, Ph.D., Bronx Zoo/Wildlife Conservation Park; Glenn Phillips, The New York Botanical Garden; **Literacy Specialist:** Maria Utefsky, Reading Recovery Coordinator, District 2, New York City

Design: MKR Design, Inc.

Photo Research: Barbara Scott

Endnotes: Susan Russell

Photographs: Cover: John Guistina/The Wildlife Collection; p. 1: Jany Sauvanet/Photo Researchers, Inc.; p. 2 (inset): G.I. Bernard/Animals, Animals; pp. 2-3: Gary Retherford/Photo Researchers, Inc.; p. 4 (inset): Tony Tilford/Oxford Scientific/Animals, Animals; pp. 4-5: Kjell B. Sandved/Butterfly Alphabet; p. 6: Jack Swenson/The Wildlife Collection; p. 7: David Northcott/DRK Photo; pp. 8-9: Michael Fodgen/Animals, Animals; p. 9 (inset) Tom Brakefield/DRK Photo; p. 10 (l): George Holton/Photo Researchers, Inc.; pp. 10 (r), 11(l & r): Carroll Henderson; p. 12: John Guistina/The Wildlife Collection.

Library of Congress Cataloging-in-Publication Data
Canizares, Susan, 1960-
Rainforest colors / Susan Canizares, Betsey Chessen.
p. cm. -- (Science emergent readers)
"Scholastic early childhood."
Includes index.
Summary: Photographs and simple text explore the unusual colorso birds, plants, and frogs in the Amazon rainforest.
ISBN 0-590-76962-6 (pbk.: alk. paper)
1. Color--Juvenile literature. 2. Rain forest ecology--Juvenile literature. [1. Color. 2. Rain forest ecology. 3. Ecology.]
I. Chessen, Betsey, 1970-. II. Title. III. Series.
QC495.5.C36 1998

535.6--dc21   97-34201
                                                                                 CIP AC

20 19 18 17 16 15 14 13 12 11   03   02   01   00

red bird

red plant

red frog

yellow **bird**

yellow plant

yellow frog

blue **bird**

blue plant

blue frog

red, yellow, blue

red, yellow, blue

red, yellow, blue, and green!

Rainforest Colors

The colors that can be found on the wildlife and the plants of the rainforest are often very vivid. In fact, the tropical rainforest is the most colorful habitat in the world. The colors that you see have different functions. Sometimes they conceal and sometimes they advertise the presence of those that are wearing them. The Scarlet Ibis (right) doesn't need to hide as it wades in the shallow water with its long legs, hunting fish, frogs, and reptiles.

Red is a color that gets a lot of attention! The Passionflower (left) needs to be noticed by the birds and insects that will carry its pollen to other plants so that its life cycle can be completed. The Poison Dart Frog (right) is red to send out a clear warning that it is poisonous and dangerous. That keeps it safe from predators.

The Golden Tanager (left) is from a large family of birds that contains over 200 species. Together, they are the most brilliantly colored of all the songbird families. The tanagers live high in the rainforest's canopy. The bright Cassia plant (right) produces beans that feed the birds and reptiles.

Blue is another standout color. For frogs, like the Gladiator Frog (left), this color says "beware" to predators. The brilliant blue of the Hyacinth Macaw (right) is just one of the bright colors that this family of birds wears. The macaws are the most vividly colored of all birds.

The Giant Bromeliad (left) attracts bugs and birds to the tiny pools of rainwater that collect in the cups that its leaves make. The Blue Poison Frog's (right) bright color warns all of its danger. The people of the rainforest dip their hunting darts into its poison.

The brilliant colors on these pages demonstrate the rich rainbow to be found in the rainforest. The Scarlet Macaw and the Passion flower (left) and the Allamanda and the Morpho Peleides Butterfly (right) show the amazing variety of plant and wildlife hues.